# 77 WAYS TO GET MORE CUSTOMERS

A catalogue record for this book is available from The British Library

# ABOUT CHRIS CARDELL

Chris Cardell is a world-renowned authority on Entrepreneur success, Online Marketing and Advanced Thinking, and trusted advisor to over 300,000 business owners worldwide.

For two decades, Chris has been working with business owners with the core focus of increasing their profits by 100% to 300%. He has been featured on the BBC, ITV, News At Ten, Sky News, LBC Radio, and featured in The Observer, The Guardian, The Mail on Sunday, and The Sunday Times. Every year, Entrepreneurs pay up to £2000 ($2500) to attend his Entrepreneur Summit, where he's shared the platform with leaders in their fields like Sir Bob Geldof, Paul McKenna, and the stars of Dragons Den.

Chris Cardell has pioneered the development of Internet Marketing for Entrepreneurs and is one of the world's leading trainers on Google, Facebook, and Online Traffic and Conversion strategies. He's helped thousands strengthen their existing businesses, and add enough extra profits to those businesses to go from struggling to paying bills to taking home tens of thousands in profit every month – by adding his advanced marketing and online strategies.

He's spent £5 million ($7.5 million) of his own money just on pay-per-click advertising on Google, Facebook, YouTube and Display advertising, so he's actually doing what he shares with you.

Chris Cardell is one of the world's highest-paid public speakers. His public events attract hundreds from across Europe and the world who experience business, financial and life transformations as a result.

Alongside his work in the Entrepreneurial world, Chris has also emerged as a leading global authority on Advanced Thinking – the culmination of the leading-edge breakthroughs of recent years on how the mind works and how to duplicate the success strategies of top achievers. Chris shows people how to use the power of the unconscious mind and fine tune their thinking for extraordinary achievement – in business and in life.

Chris's company, Cardell Media, is now one of the world's fastest growing Digital Marketing Agencies. Cardell Media works with growing businesses of all types, looking after their key Online Marketing activities. The Cardell Media Website and Internet Marketing Partnership' gives clients a world class website, online video, production and social media presence. The Cardell Media 'Google Ads and Online Advertising Partnership' manages all the Google Pay-per-Click Advertising for businesses of every type, across the world.

This book takes the best of the best of Chris's profit-generating methods, with 77 of the world's most powerful strategies to get more customers, grow your business, and increase your profits.

Chris Cardell with Robert De Niro

Chris Cardell with Martha Stewart

Every year, 800 business owners pay £2000/$2500 to attend Chris Cardell's Entrepreneur Summit

# 1: YOUR CUSTOMER GOLDMINE — UNCONVERTED LEADS

If I came into your business today, what's the very first thing I would do to get more customers into your business? I would focus on your unconverted leads. I promise that you have gold sitting in your business in what's known as your unconverted leads.

An unconverted lead is somebody who has contacted you and shown interest in what you have to sell, but they have not bought yet. We call them 'leads.' They've either contacted you via your website, or phoned you, or emailed you, or come into your premises, or made some kind of contact with you and expressed interest in what you have to offer, but they have not followed through and bought yet.

The big mistake people make is assuming that because somebody doesn't buy from you today, this week, or this month, they're never going to buy from you. It's a mistake that could be costing you a fortune.

Why do we give up on potential customers so quickly? It makes no sense. You know from your own behaviour as a consumer that you might first enquire about a product or service weeks, months, or years before you buy.

Business owners quite rightly want to know how to use the internet, Facebook, Google, social media, etc. to get customers. But before you spend anything on getting new customers, it is insane to not go to the people who've already raised their hand and told you they are interested in what you sell.

In times of Recession like we're in right now following the Coronavirus crisis, it's also very important that you find ways of getting customers that don't cost anything. We call that 'Marketing for Free,' and it's a critical Recession Immunisation strategy. It costs nothing to email or ideally phone all of your unconverted leads from the last couple of years. You will be surprised at how many lead to a sale.

Of course, if you don't have a way of keeping or 'capturing' the information from potential customers when they enquire with you, that needs sorting urgently.

When your accountant does your returns every year, they will talk to you about the 'assets' in your business. What they don't realise is that one of the most valuable assets you have are your unconverted leads. They are almost certainly worth tens if not hundreds of thousands to you. So go and mine the gold!

# 2: MAKE SURE THAT YOUR WEBSITE IS NOT DESTROYING YOUR BUSINESS

If you're frustrated at your website, if it's not getting the sales and customers you deserve, if you get traffic to your website but that traffic doesn't convert to buyers – trust me – you are not alone.

The best-kept secret in business is that virtually everybody hates their websites.

They hate their websites because their websites don't make them enough money.

The sites don't make enough money because we've all been sold a massive lie by the web design industry.

The lie is:

## *'Build it and they will come.'*

In other words, the web designers tell you that if you just build a site that looks good, with great design, the customers will follow.

Nice idea.

Only problem is, as you may have discovered, it doesn't work. It's BS.

I can show you hundreds of really good-looking websites that went out of business because they didn't do the number-one thing that all successful websites must do:

They didn't convert the visitor to a buyer.

They were websites built around the concept of design, not the concept of conversion.

I've caused lots of controversy with my comments over the years about the web design industry. But I don't care. I've had enough of seeing the lives of hard-working business owners destroyed because their websites – the single most important source of customers for all of us – let them down.

I've actually got nothing against web designers. All the ones I've met are very nice people. But the clue is in their job description:

Web 'DESIGNERS'

They understand 'Design'. They do not, in most cases, understand 'CONVERSION.'

Of course you want a nicely designed website. But that doesn't get you customers. You need a website that converts visitors to buyers.

The person running your online marketing (ideally you) needs to be a world-class expert on website conversion. By the time you've finished this book, you will be.

In the meantime, please understand that the future of your business, your financial future probably depends on your website's ability to convert.

Have a think about this:

I'm assuming you went into business to achieve financial freedom for you and those you care about.

If that's the case, that freedom is obviously only going to come from the money in your bank account.

That money is going to come from your customers.

I think we can all agree that in today's world, everyone who becomes a customer is either going to come directly from your website, or they're at least going to check out your website before buying. So your website is going to play the key role in 'converting' them to a customer.

In other words, your website determines how many customers you have, which determines your income, which determines your financial future.

So it's no exaggeration to say that your website could be destroying your business if it's not being run properly by someone who know what they're doing.

We'll come back to your website shortly but first, we need to urgently address this crazy world we're living in:

# 3: AVOID THE WORST MISTAKE YOU CAN MAKE IN A RECESSION

The next few paragraphs might well save your business from disaster. They refer to the most important thing you must do in a Recession.

This would also seem a good point to introduce myself properly. I avoided long introductions at the beginning of this book because I just wanted to get on with it. But I want you to know who I am because if you know I'm the 'real deal,' you're more likely to appreciate how powerful the strategies in this book are – and you're more likely to implement them and see great results.

My name is Chris Cardell. For more than 20 years, I've been one of the world's leading providers of Marketing, Online Marketing and business success information to Entrepreneurs across the world. 322,000 business owners have opted into my email list and receive my success tips every week. I've been featured extensively on global media, and every year, 800 business owners pay $2500 / £2000 to attend my three-day Entrepreneur Summit.

I'm globally renowned for showing business owners of every type – B2C, B2B, people selling products, people selling services – how to increase their profits by 100% to 250%.

My company, Cardell Media, is one of the world's fastest growing Digital Marketing Agencies. We manage the websites and Online Marketing for business owners in the UK, Europe, USA, Canada, Australia, and New Zealand.

So that's the quick biog. But here's the bit about me that I really want you to know because it is particularly relevant for the current global economic crisis:

Of all the work I've done with business owners like yourself over the last two decades, the thing I am most proud of is steering thousands of Entrepreneurs successfully through the last recession.

We learnt some tough lessons in the Great Recession of 2008 – 2010, but we came out of it stronger.

The most important thing we learnt – the absolute golden rule of surviving a Recession – is this:

## *In a Recession, you must NOT stop your Marketing.*

It's the single biggest mistake that nearly all businesses make. During the current crisis, 90% of your competitors will stop all of their Marketing. In many cases, this will destroy their businesses.

I urge you, implore you. Please don't do it.

I understand the pressure to cut costs. It would seem to make logical sense to stop your Marketing. When cash flow is extremely tight, we have to cut costs.

Here's the problem with that:

**www.CardellMedia.com**

Marketing is not a cost. It's the investment you make in getting customers and securing the future of your business and your financial future.

If someone had life insurance and was looking to cut personal costs during the Recession, would you recommend that they stop paying for their life insurance?

Of course not. You'd sell the car and the kids before you jeopardised your financial future by having no life insurance.

It's the same with your Marketing. Marketing is the process of getting customers. As discussed earlier, your financial future depends on it. You do not want to stop the one thing that is going to protect that future.

Here's what happened to many of the businesses who stopped their Marketing during the last Recession:

They actually survived the worst part of the Recession. They cut costs so dramatically they were able to keep going for a while.

Then, when the economy started picking up, they realised they weren't just out of cash, they were also out of customers.

They had stopped all of their customer communication for months and months.

So as the economy picked up and they looked for business, there was none because there was no backlog of pent-up customer demand to fall back on.

That's when, sadly, most went out of business.

I understand the financial pressures during this Recession. It's one of the reasons I'm making this book available Free. And it's packed with strategies that will reduce your costs substantially.

It's also packed with numerous 'Marketing for Free' strategies.

So please, whatever you do, you must avoid the number-one mistake people make in a Recession:

You must not stop your Marketing.

# 4: YOUR WEBSITE MUST PASS THE 8 SECOND TEST

Here's one of the most important facts that you should know about Online Marketing:

50% of website visitors leave the typical website within 8 seconds.

That fact should drive your entire approach to your website and online marketing.

Because of the nature of surfing the web – going from one site to another to another – it should come as no surprise that on average, 50% of people are gone from most websites within 8 seconds.

But if that includes your website, we've got a major challenge, particularly if you're paying for some of that traffic.

It means that your website must be different from the rest.

It means that your website must do something to get your visitors to STOP and stay on your website rather than surfing the web.

So we've got to do something at the top of your home page or key landing pages to grab your visitors' attention and keep them on your site.

Which brings us to one of the best ways to achieve that:

# 5: ONLINE VIDEO

One of the best ways to make sure that your website passes the 8 second test and getting your website visitors to stop and stay on your site is by using Online Video.

If you look at how the internet is moving and developing, websites as we've known them up to now are starting to morph into multimedia sites. The thing we refer to as the internet is becoming more of a multimedia environment. The boundary between your internet experience and your television experience is starting to disappear. It's all starting to merge together. Five years from now, a business's website won't feel like a website. It will feel almost like a mini TV channel or certainly a mini multimedia experience.

Online video is crucial in this downturn. Firstly, it's close to free. You just need a decent phone – and, ideally, a lapel microphone. If you want to be more professional, you can also order an iPhone tripod which means you get steady footage. Next, Online Video is crucial in this economy because it builds the relationship with your customer.  Nothing is more important right now than bonding with your customers. Video lets you do that.

There are two main ways of doing Online video. The first is you looking at the camera and speaking to the camera, just like you see on the TV news. If you are comfortable doing that, great. It gives authority and will capture your viewer's attention.

Not everyone is comfortable talking to a camera. That's fine too. If that's the case, just have someone interview you and ask the five or six most commonly asked questions in your business.

When it's being filmed, ignore the camera and just chat to the person asking the questions.

You can then edit that video into five or six separate videos – one for each answer.

Put your new videos on your website, email them to your customers, put them on social media, and upload into your YouTube channel.

# 6: YOU MUST HAVE A MOBILE FIRST WEBSITE AND BUSINESS

Mobile website traffic is now ranging from 60% to 70%, meaning that 60% to 70% of your website traffic is likely to be coming from people on a Mobile device.

This means that you need what we a call a 'Mobile First' website and business.

Mobile First means that your entire Marketing should be built around serving people on mobile.

You probably designed your current website understandably imagining people looking at it on a computer. That's certainly what I did until recently.

But now we have to imagine them on a phone.

Mobile First is not the same as 'Mobile Friendly' A Mobile Friendly site just refers to a site that technically functions ok on a phone.

Mobile First involves thinking about the behaviour of the customer and the environment they're in. For example, someone at home or in the office on a desktop computer has time and space to carefully look at your website and read its pages.

But the person looking at your website on a phone in a café, or on the train, or at home watching TV will make a decision about your site in moments and is very easily distracted.

So our Mobile First website will be aiming to capture their attention fast, possible with Online Video or some of the other strategies we're going to cover.

It's not just your website. 'Mobile First' applies to all of your Marketing. For example, when you email your customers, we need to remember that most will be opening those emails on a phone, and if we send them to a web page from that email, we need to think about both the action we want that customer to take – and the context and physical environment they're in when making that decision.

# 7: THE VITAL IMPORTANCE OF PAGE LOAD SPEED

Google estimates that for every extra second your web pages take to download, your conversion rate (the percentage of web visitors who convert to a customer) drops by 20%.

Bear in mind that Google is basing this on the huge amount of data they see going through both their advertising system and Google Analytics.

It's a terrifying statistic. Every extra second your website takes to download could be losing you another 20% of sales and profits.

Part of my business involves building and managing websites that convert for my customers, so my team and I look at hundreds of websites every year. One of the major problems is that their sites don't load fast enough.

This can be because of your hosting, or how your website has been built, or both. It's why your decision about who is going to manage your website and Online Marketing going forward is one of the most important you'll make.

There's another more subtle benefit from improving your page load speeds:

If you do pay-per-click advertising on Google, one of the key components of success is your Quality Score, which is a score from 1 – 10 that Google gives all of your keywords.

Put simply, the higher your Quality Score, the cheaper your cost per click and the higher up the page you'll appear.

One of the key elements that Google looks at when deciding your Quality Score is the load time of the pages you're sending traffic to.

So the faster your pages load, the higher your Quality Score, and the more successful your Google campaigns will be.

# 8: PUT YOUR PHONE NUMBER EVERYWHERE

The fact that 60% to 70% of your website visitors are likely to be on Mobile is a major challenge. But it's also a big opportunity.

These customers are holding a phone in their hands. So how about getting them to call you.

All you've got to do is convince them to tap their phone and they're through to you for a potential sale.

This is a major overlooked opportunity. People forget that, before the internet, the telephone was the number-one sales tool for anyone in business.

It was the best option because if you can speak to someone, there's a much higher chance of them buying – and they'll often spend more than someone you don't get the chance to speak to.

So your website should have your phone number EVERYWHERE.

On mobile it should be an easy tap to call button and it should repeat several times on your main pages.

With our client websites, we use a technology that has a 'sticky' tap to call button that stays at the bottom of your screen as you scroll down the page. It's very effective.

# 9: SEND MORE EMAILS

It's very simple.

If you want more customers and sales, send more emails.

Although you and I may not have met yet, I can predict with certainty that you're not sending enough emails.

How do I know this? Because hardly anyone is sending enough emails.

Here's a key fact for you:

The average email open rate is 20%.

That means that to reach 100% of your customers, you would need, on average, to send five emails.

Or to put it another way, if you're only sending one email each month, it's going to take you five months to reach all of your customers.

You must get your customers used to receiving at least two or three emails each week.

The secret to doing that successfully is not to bombard them with sales messages. Some of your emails should just be packed with useful information, or tips and advice, or links to your social media posts, or links to your online videos.

When you do that, your customers actually end up looking forward to receiving your emails and are more than happy if some of them make them an offer or encourage a sale.

Business owners are sometimes hesitant to send more emails because they're worried about people unsubscribing. I actually encourage people to unsubscribe.

I send emails every day to my customers. They are packed with useful information. My work is all about providing the greatest strategies in the world for Entrepreneurs who want to be at the leading edge of human excellence. If people don't want that info, that's fine with me. They can and should unsubscribe.

My business is a search for champions, and I suggest that yours should be too.

The search for champions is the search for people who are going to be great, long-term customers.

For me, those are the highly success-driven business owners who are seriously committed to at least doubling their profits. I'm likely to have relationships with these customers for the next 5 or 10 years or more.

You will have your own equivalent to that.

Such a customer is going to be more than happy to receive frequent emails from you – and you should be willing to let the rest go.

The other reason you should be sending more emails is that it's FREE.

Marketing for Free is good in the best of times. During this Recession, it's essential.

So please, send more emails!

# 10: MAKE SURE YOUR EMAILS ARE OPENED

How do you get your emails opened? You do that primarily with the title of your email. The title of your email is the most important part of your email. It's like a headline in a newspaper ad. It determines whether the customer is going to read the rest of the email.

If you look down your inbox at the emails you get from businesses, they tend to have unbelievably boring titles, and that's why so many business emails aren't opened. "A 10 per cent price saving" is not an exciting email title.

If you look at the titles of the emails I send, they are hopefully either interesting, intriguing, funny, or controversial. I'll do whatever it takes it to get people to read the email. When an email comes into your inbox, you're going to be selective about the ones you open, so you must use creative titles in your email.

# 11: BUILD A LARGE EMAIL LIST

People often ask me how I went from zero to building a multimillion pound/dollar global business.

There are several factors, but there's one thing I am sure of.

I couldn't have done it without building a large email list.

Over the years, over 300,000 business owners have opted in to my email lists, or purchased products from me, or requested resources such as this book.

That email list is one of the most valuable assets in my business.

Of course, you don't need an email list anything like that size. You can make good money from a list of prospects with just a couple hundred people in it.

But it is vital that you do everything you can to build a good email list.

Here are just some of the sources for your email list:

1. Customers
2. Website visitors
3. People who phone you with enquiries
4. People who email you with enquiries
5. People who fill out contact forms on your website
6. Referrals

7. Traffic from Google
8. Traffic from Facebook
9. People who request guides or reports from your website
10. Social Media

If you don't already have one, you'll need an Auto Responder on your website, which is the technology that lets you capture peoples' contact details.

Also, to be clear, I am only talking about permission-based email marketing from people who have specifically opted in with you. I am not referring to renting email lists or scraping the internet for email addresses which is completely ineffective at best and – depending where you are located – legally questionable at worst.

Build an email list with people who want to engage with you, and you will have a source of income and profits for years to come.

# 12: GIVE, GIVE, GIVE

Here's an alternative take on business that might just change your Entrepreneurial life.

Most business owners wait until their customers give them money before adding any value to those customers lives..

I say "Why wait?"

If you want to not just survive this Recession but come out of it thriving, you're only going to do that by creating extraordinary relationships with your customers.

The first step to an extraordinary relationship is your customers knowing that you truly care about them.

I'm giving business owners Free access to this book during the Recession because I genuinely care about their wellbeing. That's not B.S. The Entrepreneurs of the world have been my life for the last two decades. I may not have all the answers, but I know for a fact that I have knowledge and strategies that can be a huge help to their businesses and – to be blunt – in many cases during this crisis, can save their businesses.

I also know that helping these Entrepreneurs is not just about business. Their entire financial wellbeing of them and their their families is linked to their business surviving this chaos.

So the first reason I'm giving is because it's just the right thing to do.

The second reason is because it's the right approach for my business too.

For example, I have a number of Private Clients who pay me £5000 or $7000 per month for me to effectively be their Marketing Director, have me run their Marketing, and my team implement it all, from Marketing planning to advanced Google, Facebook or ecommerce campaigns.

I know from experience that at some point in the future, some of the people reading this book will use its contents to turn their business around, make a lot of money as a result, and will then end up wanting to be a Private Client.

So giving and making money are not mutually exclusive. In fact, they are eminently compatible.

I urge you, during these challenging times for many of your customers, to step into their shoes and think about how you can help them. It could be by giving them resources. It could be by giving them a payment break. It could be as simple as phoning them up to see how they're doing.

I've been privileged over the last 20 years to spend time with many multimillionaire Entrepreneurs. Without exception, money is not their main motivator.

They love money and profits. It's important to them, and so it should be.

But it's not their main driver.

Their main driver is impacting peoples' lives.

One of the reasons they're so wealthy is they've learned that if they just focus and obsess about that – about making a difference to their customers' lives, the money will follow.

# 13: GUARANTEES

If you want more customers, guarantee what you sell.

It's as simple and straightforward as that.

You should have strong, compelling guarantees throughout all your marketing and advertising.

If somebody spends money with you and they absolutely hate what you do for them, chances are you'll probably give them a refund or partial refund, depending on what you're selling.

Given that's the case, you want to be explicit about that. You want to make it a core part of your marketing message. On your website and marketing material, guarantees should be everywhere. Trust is important, and it sells.

If you want to know whether Guarantees will work for your business, just test it and do the maths.

It's not unusual to see a 30% to 40% increase in sales by offering a powerful guarantee.

But people always say, "What if everyone asks for a refund?" First of all, they won't.

Second, as I say. Test it and see for yourself.

If a Guarantee increases your sales by 30% and you get a 5% refund rate, you are laughing all the way to the bank.

I always tell people to offer guarantees, but in this economy, it becomes much more important.

You need to eliminate the perceived risk in your customers' minds when they're deciding whether to spend money with you.

Guarantees achieve that and send a very powerful message about your confidence in what you sell.

When I do my big 3-day Entrepreneur Summits which cost up to £2000 or $2000, I tell people that if by lunchtime on the first day, they've not already mastered strategies that will be worth 10K to them, they can leave and get a full refund. The most we've ever had leave, out of 800 in the room, is 3.

I can make such a powerful guarantee because I know how effective what I have is for my customers. Assuming that you are in the same position, you can do the same.

It's very simple. The more powerful the guarantee, the higher the sales.

# 14: DON'T STOP COMMUNICATING TO YOUR CUSTOMERS DURING THE RECESSION — EVEN IF THEY CAN'T BUY

Do you care about your customers? If you do, why would you stop communicating to them just because they can't give you money right now?

The business owner who ignores their customers during this time is telling them they view their relationship as purely transactional: When the money stops, the relationship stops.

People aren't stupid. They'll remember this, and they'll treat those business owners accordingly when the time comes.

Meanwhile, if you take the time and trouble to keep communicating with your customers, you will be rewarded. It's also just the right thing to do.

So if they're able to buy from you, step up the marketing and customer communication: Emails, Facebook, even Direct Mail if it's feasible.

If they can't currently buy, just get in touch with your customers and see how they're doing. Nobody bothers doing that, and it will blow their minds. So email them, call them, text them Do the right thing and you will be rewarded.

# 15: FACEBOOK REMARKETING

Remarketing is an incredibly effective way to keep in front of your customers and leads.

Until Remarketing, if someone came to your website and then left without buying or contacting you, they were lost forever.

But those days are over.

Here's how Remarketing works on Facebook (you can also do it on Google and YouTube as we'll discover).

Let's say I visit your website one afternoon. I have a look around and leave. I'm interested in what you sell but for whatever reason, I don't make contact straight away.

Your page has a piece of code on it from Facebook. This means that Facebook now knows I've been to your website.

So when I go onto Facebook that evening, what's the first thing that appears in my newsfeed?

A post about you and your business. Technically it's a sponsored post that you're paying for, but it looks just like a normal post and contains a line to your website, or video, or whatever you choose.

As a customer, I'm blown away. And it's incredibly cheap for you because you're only paying to reach the people who come to your site.

To do this you need to set up a Facebook advertising account. It's well worth the effort, and we see great results with Facebook Remarketing.

# 16: GOOGLE REMARKETING

You can also do Remarketing with banner ads through Google's Display network.

If you've ever been looking at a website and seen banner ads for a business that you're a customer of, that's Remarketing.

It's the same principle as with Facebook. Google partners with millions of websites for its banner ads 'Display Network.'

So I come to your website, the Google code is on the site, I leave your website, and later I go to a website such as a news site or sports site, and I see a banner ad for your business.

The power of this is that I start to get a sense that you are everywhere.

Of course, to me, you are everywhere. But again, it's only me and people who've been to your site who are seeing these ads. So it's very targeted and very cost effective.

Your Google Remarketing ads are run through your Google Ads account (formerly Google AdWords) the same account where you run your Pay-per-Click ads on Google.

# 17: YOUTUBE REMARKETING

Remarketing on YouTube is one of my favourite strategies. So I visit your website, then tomorrow I go onto YouTube and search for something of interest.

Before my video starts, a video about you and your business plays.

How cool is that!

And here's the best part.

On the bottom right of your video is a button that says 'Skip Ad.' If I don't want to watch your video and click the Skip add button, you don't pay anything.

We've found that on average, 25% to 35% of people choose to keep watching.

On your video you can direct them to your website and include any message you choose.

Even better, YouTube doesn't care how long your video is. It can be 30 seconds, 2 minutes, 5 minutes or more. You don't pay anything extra, and you can reach people this way on YouTube for pennies.

Because YouTube is owned by Google, your YouTube remarketing is run through your Google Ads account.

NOTE: Remarketing on Facebook, Google, and YouTube, along with Pay-per-Click advertising on Google is complicated and should be managed by someone who know what they are doing. At my company, Cardell Media, we have a 50 strong team managing the online marketing for business owners across the world.

**Go to the contact page at www.CardellMedia.com and we'll be happy to help.**

# 18: REFERRALS

One of the best ways to grow a highly successful business is through Referrals – people who come to you through word-of-mouth recommendation from an existing customer.

Customers who come through Referrals are the best customers you can get. First of all, they're FREE. Secondly, they tend to be your best spending customers. They spend more with you than a normal customer because they come through the door to feel good about you because someone has recommended you to them.

Here's the big secret of success with Referrals.

Pretty much everybody gets referrals. But almost without exception, the referrals are accidental. In other words, the business owner does nothing to get them, other than providing a good product or service to the customers they have. They are in no way being proactive in getting referrals.

You need to ask for Referrals.

If you're getting Referrals at the moment without asking for them, what would happen if you proactively asked for them.

You need to have a system in place for getting Referrals. The absolute first thing you want to do is have a referral culture in your business. A referral culture involves your customers understanding that referrals are a core part of how you grow.

So have a conversation with your customers when they first become a customer of yours. You can say, "I build my business primarily through word-of-mouth recommendation with individuals like yourself. If I do a great job for you, would you be willing to recommend me to friends, family, and colleagues?"

Who's going to say no to that?

This might seem like a small point, but here's what I've seen over the years.

If business has one in ten of its customers bringing in referrals, without trying, when they proactively ask, that number can go up to three or four or five out of ten.

That's an increase in Referrals of 200% to 400%. Scale that out across the year and it can transform a business.

Just putting that concept of Referrals in peoples' heads, literally implanting that idea in their mind, will increase referrals on its own. If every customer that became a customer of yours next week brought one person into your business, and then that person brought one more person into your business, you'd never have to do any marketing or advertising again. That is the sheer power of referrals.

# 19: REFERRAL MARKETING CAMPAIGNS

People generally accept that they should have marketing campaigns in their business, meaning you promote a specific product or service, and you have a marketing campaign that consists of things you send through emails, a website, online videos etc. You may also call or go to see your customers to get sales. That's a marketing campaign in a nutshell.

But just as importantly, you also need a marketing campaign purely for Referrals.

Send your existing customers to a page on your website asking for referrals. Perhaps offer rewards, bonuses, or vouchers if they give you a referral. Why wouldn't you send emails to your customers two or three times a year asking for this? You can send a letter to your 100 best customers for somewhere between 50 and 100 pounds or dollars. Why wouldn't you do that a couple of times a year if that brought in 3, 6, or 19 new customers?

So you want to have what we call an 'Internal' Marketing campaign. You want to have an Internal Referral marketing campaign running across the year to get you the Referrals you need.

# 20: REWARD YOUR CUSTOMERS FOR REFERRALS

When your customers refer a new customer to you, you should reward them.

First, it's the right thing to do. Second, if your customers learn that they get a reward for recommending you, they'll do it again and again.

The form of that reward or 'thank you' depends partly on the business that you are in and what you're selling.

The best type of reward is the cash reward, for obvious reasons. People like money! If it's appropriate to do this, you should consider it.

A close relative of the cash reward is the gift or gift certificate. So you could send your referring customer a bottle of champagne, or if you sell products – one of your products. Or a gift certificate for a local business or restaurant.

In some businesses, rewards that have financial value are not allowed. In these cases, you should at least thank the person with a handwritten note. I am sure you recommend people to various businesses all the time. When did the owner of one of those businesses last send you a personal thank you? Probably never.

Hopefully you are getting a sense of how powerful these strategies are. Imagine having an internal Marketing system for getting Referrals, loads of Referrals coming in, those people referring you being rewarded, and doing it again and again. Then the icing on the cake – the people coming into your business through Referrals start recommending you and getting Referrals too.

It's a very powerful spiral of success that can transform your business.

# 21: SUPPLIER REFERRALS

Here's a great Referral strategy.

Don't just get Referrals from your customers. Get them from your suppliers too.

You want to find out who your suppliers know who could also be potential customers of yours. Establish a good relationship with your suppliers if you haven't already, ask the question, and get the contact details of all those untapped potential customers.

If your suppliers are smart, they will realise that it's in their best interests to help your business grow, and they could become an ongoing source of Referrals for you.

If you put the initial time in, this is a brilliant way to increase your customer base without having to spend a single penny.

# 22: SELL BENEFITS, NOT FEATURES

Make sure that all of your marketing is talking about the benefits and not the features. Not communicating the benefits is one of the fundamental marketing mistakes that many people make.

If I want to buy a new Hi-Fi and the salesperson starts telling me about how many decibel levels are coming out of the woofer and that it took 19 hours to make in Taiwan, unless I'm a complete Hi-Fi geek, I really couldn't care less. They're just listing me the features, not the benefits. The benefits are that this is going to look lovely in my home. It's going to produce amazing sound. I'm going to listen to my favourite music and it's going to feel like I'm right there in the heart of the concert venue where it's taking place.

You need to know what is important to your customer. Some people will buy a Hi-Fi because it will impress the neighbours. If that's your customer's thing, you need to focus on that. You must sell the benefits and not the features.

If you're selling hammers, you're not selling a hammer or even the hole in the wall; you're selling the ability to put an amazing picture, photo, or painting on the wall and give that person a wonderful experience every time they look at it. That's the benefit the hammer offers.

Look at all of your marketing, particularly areas such as the home page of your website. You need to start telling your customers about the benefits within the first one or two sentences. Benefits not features!

# 23: IMPROVE YOUR SALES SKILLS

If you really want to become superb at getting customers, you really must understand and be able to practise the art of it, the slightly intangible element of sales.

Your ability to sell effectively is as important to your ability to get customers as anything else, and it always will be. If you have a team around you, the same obviously applies for your team.

I highlight this because most business owners don't go into business to sell. They don't think, "I'd like to leave this lousy job I'm in and spend all day selling things to people," because most people don't particularly like the idea of selling. You normally go into business because you really want to get out of the job you're in, or you're really motivated to carry out a service or offer a particular product. As I'm sure you've realised by now, this is nowhere near enough to be successful. Everything in your business success boils down to just two things. Sales and Marketing.

Whether you're growing a huge company or starting a local business from your back bedroom, you are an Entrepreneur. As an Entrepreneur, you have to get great at selling, not just so you yourself can sell but so that you can also make sure the key people on your team are also doing it well.

There are all sorts of ways to improve your sales skills. You can take courses, read books, and attend seminars, but my core message to you is that you need to understand the fundamental importance of sales as part of the customer attraction and acquisition strategy within your business.

George Foreman, the two-time world heavyweight champion, Olympic gold medallist, and Entrepreneur, said that if he could teach his children one thing in life, it would be to sell because then, in his words, "They will always be able to pay the mortgage."

Also, in this economic environment, the blunt truth is that those that can sell will survive and those that can't, won't.

So start to become fascinated with the art and science of selling.

# 24: OVERCOME OBJECTIONS

One of the key sales skills is to know how to overcome objections from your customers.

An interesting question to ask about your potential customers is this:

Why would somebody go to the trouble of inquiring about your business, filling in a form on your website, or picking up the phone to call you and then not buy? They're obviously interested in what you're selling. Assuming what you have is of good value and meets their needs, why wouldn't the figure be 100 per cent?

The answer is customer objections. The thing that stops a sale happening is rarely that you don't have what a customer needs or wants.  Normally, there's an objection in your customer's head.

Most objections are about money, trust, and time. "It's too expensive," is a big objection. "I don't believe this will work for me" is another. "I don't have time to invest in doing this" would be another objection. You're also going to have objections specific to your business.

You need to become very clear on what your customers' objections are and come up with clear answers to those objections.

List them one by one and work out the best answers to those objections. There will only be three or four objections that you hear all the time. Get really good at answering those and you will see a significant increase in your sales.

# 25: TEACH ALL OF YOUR TEAM HOW TO SELL

Everyone in your business who communicates to customers is a salesperson.

Everyone in your business who communicates to customers can make more sales happen.

The scary part is everyone in your business who talks to customers can also stop the sale happening.

I recently bought a £1000/$1200 product and called the company's customer service department with a question about the product that I needed sorting. The first thing they asked me was if I wanted a refund!  The owner of that business needs to realise that their customer service people are sales people. They can influence the sale and a good place to start would be by not trying to reverse the sale.

We call this the sales prevention department. If you employ people who talk to customers, you need to make sure they're not managing your sales prevention department.

This is a major problem in growing businesses. It's made worse by the fact that some employees resent you, the Entrepreneur. They think you're 'lucky.'  They haven't the beginnings of an idea what it took to create your success. They won't bring up their resentment to your face, but they will end up either consciously or subconsciously sabotaging your sales.

Anyone in your business who communicates to customers' needs training, and they need policing. You should be able to listen to customer service calls, and if you really want to see how much money you're losing, you should have people cold call your business and record the calls. I warn you in advance, it can be a painful experience but not doing it is like avoiding a trip to the dentist because your tooth hurts. The problem ain't going away by ignoring it.

So everyone in your business who talks to customers is a salesperson. If you think the receptionist who answers your phone isn't a salesperson involved in the sales process, you'll want to think again. Anybody involved in the sales process needs to be trained in how to sell and ideally compensated in a way that is linked to the sales.

# 26: USE DIRECT MAIL

For over 100 years, Direct Mail has been a highly effective way of getting customers into any business, but it's not used by growing businesses anything like as much as it should be.

Everyone is excited about the internet, and I love the internet, but it's not either/or. Until the internet came along, Direct Mail was the main way of getting customers in many businesses, particularly Business to Business and retail.

Assuming that the internet replaced that is a big mistake. It didn't replace it. It complemented it.

In my company, we engage in some of the world's most sophisticated internet marketing. We send hundreds of emails each year, spend millions on Google and Facebook, test hundreds of online videos, and at any one time are testing several hundred different landing pages.

So why is it also the case that I spend hundreds of thousands each year on Direct Mail? It would be much easier to just send another email, rather than getting something printed and posted to my customers.

I do it because I know that the challenge of getting the sale in this cluttered media and online environment is a significant one. A lot of that can be done on the internet, but there is a big proportion of the population who still value and want something physical to look at, understand, and literally hold in their hands before they give you money.

This applies more as your price point goes up. If you're selling for 4.95, it's much easier to do it online. Once you get past 100 or 200 pounds or dollars, you're into a different ball game where the use of direct mail is very effective.

The beauty of direct mail is that it's so personal. How else can you get right in front of people having a direct conversation with them, saying whatever you need to say to them, in their kitchen, lounge, or office.

Full disclosure: Using Direct Mail to get brand-new customers can be hard work. It's well worth the effort, but it can involve some trial and error. You need to be willing to try some mailings that might not work and not give up too easily. It's worth it long term because once you find an approach that works, you can use it forever.

But using Direct Mail to sell more to your existing customers is just a no-brainer. It you send a great offer to your 100 best customers and think of how much that mailing will cost – and the money you will make if you get a reasonable response, it's hard not to make money.

So my most successful Private Clients do monthly direct mail campaigns to their customers and, in most cases, it adds six or seven figures to their businesses every year.

# 27: SEND POSTCARDS

Whatever size business you have and whoever your customers are, please test sending postcards to promote what you sell.

Postcards are wonderful for a couple of reasons. Firstly, they're cheap. You don't have to pay for an envelope or pay for the envelope being stuffed. You want your postcard to be the largest size allowed for the cheapest mailing.

Secondly, not only are postcards cheap, but they have a very good readership level because the person is definitely going to see it. They don't have to do anything to read it – they don't have to open an envelope. The customer is at least going to give you the chance to get your message across.

You can test specific offers, events you're doing, or sales you're having. You can use postcards to sell to new customers or to do lead generation. You can use postcards to send people to your website. You can send postcards whether you sell to businesses or consumers. Postcards are a great way to get new customers into your business and sell more to existing customers.

# 28: TESTIMONIALS

You must use testimonials. They are a great way of getting more customers. There is a proportion of the population, around 30 to 40 per cent, for whom social proof is a key element of their buying decision. Social proof is the thinking that "Everybody else is doing this. I should do this too."

Think of the growth of Apple's products, like the iPhone. Would it be fair to say that social proof played a part in its growth?

Everybody has an iPhone. Everybody is going to the Apple Store. Social proof is important. For a good chunk of the population, it's really important to the extent that they actually won't do business with you if there isn't some social proof.

Testimonials are social proof. Having real-life stories and case studies from people who've experienced and benefited from what you've got can't fail to increase your sales, so you want testimonials on your website and any written material you have. You can even include testimonials in your emails.

If you meet customers face-to-face, one highly effective strategy is to have a book of testimonials ready to pull out. The time to pull them out is when the customer comes up with the objections we talked about earlier. "Your product is a bit expensive," to which you can reply "Can I show you something? Here are some people who also raised the issue of price, and here's what happened when they went ahead and did business with us. Here are their stories."

Use testimonials. They cost nothing to get and will increase your sales.

# 29: VIDEO TESTIMONIALS

Video testimonials are particularly powerful and effective, so it's worth going to the time and trouble to record testimonials from your customers wherever possible.

The reason that video testimonials are highly effective is that they are so believable. If you have great written testimonials, people can question their authenticity (which is why ideally you should include their full name on the testimonial). But there's no doubting the authenticity of video testimonials.

If you meet your customers in person, have a good mobile phone and lapel microphone or similar device ready to record them, with their permission of course. If you go out to them, do the same thing. If you don't have much direct contact with your customers, it's worth you or somebody else going out to them and recording these messages. Alternatively, get the customer to record the testimonials and send them to you.

You can use your video testimonials:

- On your website
- In emails with links to the video
- In your Facebook ads
- On all of your social media
- On YouTube
- As part of your Remarketing

You can, of course, also transcribe your video testimonials and use them in your written material.

# 30: DIRECT SALES

One of the best ways to get more customers is direct sales – having a salesperson or sales team go out into the real world and get sales. It's one of the obvious strategies, but everyone is very drawn to the internet and overlooks traditional selling. Many businesses would still benefit from having a person or people go out into the field.

In a growing business, transitioning from just 'Marketing' (using the type of strategies we've been discussing) to adding a sales operation to that business is one of the best ways to rapidly grow that business, often by hundreds of per cent.

There are two options when considering adding Direct Sales to your business.

The first is to have salespeople who physically visit customers.

The second is to have salespeople on the phone.

This can be a great place to start. It's generally easier to find a good telemarketer than it is a good direct sales person. It also gives you the advantage that a telemarketer does not necessarily have to be in your office or even your geographic location. Just monitor them carefully. (I recommend paying their phone bill so you can see how many calls they're making).

Of course, in this new world we're living in, there is also a combination of the two functions above where face-to-face meetings are replaced with online meetings.

# 31: PAY YOUR SALESPEOPLE A HIGH COMMISSION

It still amazes me how many businesses don't pay salespeople commission – and where they do, pay very low commission.

This varies considerably from country to country. In the USA, where I lived for several years, they understand paying commissions. I'll never forget when I first went to buy a car in California. Their salespeople are all commission only. If they don't sell, they don't get to eat. When you walk onto a forecourt, you ain't getting out until you either buy or the salespeople have died trying!

In the UK, the opposite is the case. Many salespeople are still just on salary, which is insane. Human nature is human nature. People are mostly self-serving (particularly in business) and if your salesperson is going to make more money if they get the sale, they will work harder to get the sale. That's life. That's reality. You can fight it all you want but facts are facts.

People ask, 'How much of the salary should be commission?' The answer is, 'As much as possible.'

What's interesting is that the better the salesperson, the more willing they are to be on commission and have a large part of their income commission based. They know they'll make more money that way because they know how good they are.

Lousy salespeople (and just to save you a few years of pain, most salespeople are lousy) hate the idea.

The ideal scenario is to have salespeople who are 100% commission based. That's what I have in my business. They're hard to find, but they're great for obvious reasons. You only pay when they get a sale.

My salespeople earn six figures, and I'm happy to pay them that because they're sharing in the success they create. As the owner of the business, you should be willing to pay your salespeople a lot, definitely more than the competition so that you end up with the best salespeople. The trick is to pay them for getting sales, not for turning up to work and gazing out of the window.

# 32: TELESEMINARS/WEBINARS

A teleseminar or telephone seminar is just a big conference call. You book with a conference call company. You can Google "conference calls" and book a phone system. It's normally very cheap. You can have a conference call or teleseminar with 100 people, seven people, or 500 people. We sometimes have 2,000 people on these calls. They're a great way to deliver information to more than one of your customers at the same time.

Webinars work in exactly the same way but you're on video.

If you have a small business, the nice thing is the people on the teleseminar or webinar don't know how many other people are on. Don't feel you need to attract huge numbers of people on the call.

Remember our earlier point about how there are people who have inquired about your business but are currently unconverted leads? Teleseminars and webinars work wonderfully with existing customers, but they're great for new customers as well.

All sorts of businesses can arrange a teleseminar or webinar and use it to their advantage. If you're in manufacturing, you could do a teleseminar updating customers and new potential customers on the product range that you offer. If you provide a service, like accounting, you could and should do a webinar or teleseminar a day or two after the government budget is announced to tell your customers and potential customers what's in it for them.

You can combine the customer and the new customer at the same time. You could do a teleseminar for your customers and encourage them to invite people they know. That becomes a source of referrals.

One of the things you're also going to see when implementing these 77 strategies is that once you start combining them, the sum is greater than the parts.

# 33: LIVE ONLINE MEETINGS

The world has changed and now Live Meetings are part of all our lives.

If you'd told me before the lockdown that I would be doing WhatsApp video calls with my Mum, I would have said you're crazy. But here we are all meeting online.

Many businesses are having great success by leveraging that change in behaviour and doing online meetings with their customers, either as a group or one to one.

A lot of businesses that are doing very well used to send a salesperson on a three-hour trip to meet somebody. Sometimes that's still necessary, but often they can get the same or better results by doing that meeting online. Invite the person to a video presentation online. It's an efficient way of communication, keeps costs down, and shows that you're a modern, professional business. Test this out.

# 34: FACEBOOK ADVERTISING

It is highly likely that Facebook advertising could be a game changer for your business and make you a lot of money.

In my business, for example, I get the largest number of lowest cost customers from Facebook (even though I'm in B2B and Facebook is supposed to not work in Business to Business. Trust me. It does).

There are two key things to understand about Facebook advertising. The first is its phenomenal reach. Fifty per cent of all internet users spend an average of half an hour each day on Facebook – and that's just an average. As you know, many people spend several hours each day on Facebook. Personally, I think it's a complete waste of time, but that's what people want to do.

If 50 per cent of all internet users spend half an hour each day on Facebook, that also means that 50 per cent of your customers spend half an hour a day on Facebook. In other words, your customers are on Facebook.

The second key factor is that Facebook has the ability to learn how to find you the best customers at the lowest cost. This is through a combination of its amazing targeting, based on the huge amount of information it has on all of its users – and its Artificial Intelligence and Machine Learning. To put it simply, Facebook uses its computing power and knowledge on its users to profile the people who respond to offers on your websites and then find people who behave like they do.

It then serves 'Sponsored Posts' into only the newsfeeds of people that Facebook thinks are likely to become your customers.

Sponsored Posts are normal posts that you just happen to pay to reach people. That's the other beauty of Facebook. The ads don't look like ads. They look like posts, so more people are willing to read them.

You can use Facebook Advertising whether you have a large business or a local one. In fact, Facebook is great for small local businesses as you can just run your sponsored posts to people in your area – but you still have access to all that computing power and Artificial Intelligence that larger businesses do.

# 35: USE THE POWER OF FACEBOOK LOOKALIKE AUDIENCES

Now the advanced Facebook strategies that your competitors won't have a clue about.

The most powerful tool on Facebook is its lookalike audiences.

Here's how it works.

You upload your customer list into Facebook, so names, emails – and address and phone number if you have them.

Facebook then goes through all the information it has on all of those customers (without sharing that information with you, so there are no privacy issues).

It figures out the ages, locations, demographics, likes and behaviours of your best customers.

It then goes out to its massive number of users and looks for people who look like your customers. Hence 'Lookalike audiences.'

It just serves your ads to them as it knows they are more likely to convert.

But it doesn't stop there.

Facebook's Artificial Intelligence learns which of those people convert on your website (to a lead or buyer) and keeps learning as your campaigns continue so that it's able to get you more and more customers, cheaper and cheaper.

The power of Facebook's Lookalike Audiences has to be seen to be believed. It works in Ecommerce, but it works for all types of business. For example, if you want people to contact or phone you when they get to your site, it will learn who on your site responds and contacts you, and target the rest of your campaigns towards people who look most like them and are likely to convert

**NOTE: If you want help running Facebook Advertising campaigns, including lookalike audiences, go to the contact page at www.CardellMedia.com and speak to my team.**

# 36: CONSTANTLY REFRESH YOUR FACEBOOK ADS

Unlike Google, where a successful ad can run for years without being changed (because it's a constantly new audience of searchers), on Facebook, you have to constantly update your ads.

After two or three weeks of running a campaign on Facebook, most of the audience are likely to have seen your ad.

If you keep running it, you will run into what's known as 'Ad Fatigue.' Less people will click on it and so less people will convert. It will look like your campaign has stopped working.

So always be ready with a new set of ads. On Facebook, the picture in the ad is the most important part. It's what influences people to read your post and click on it, so test different pictures and see what generates the best results. When you see the response to your ads diminishing, swap it out for a new one.

# 37: TEST VIDEO ADS ON FACEBOOK

Some of our best successes with our clients where we manage their Facebook Marketing has come from Video and Video Ads.

Remember, your sponsored post basically means that you can get your post seen by the people you want to target on Facebook.

The format of that post is up to you. Video is popular in normal posts, so you should test using it on your Facebook ads too.

If you watch people who are on Facebook, especially those on mobile phones, you will notice that they stop when they see videos. Their brains have learnt to stop and watch the videos.

That's why I said earlier that when you produce your online videos – which are essential for your website – you should also test them in your Facebook posts.

So run them in your Facebook Remarketing ads. Then if you're also trying Lookalike audiences, run them on there and see how they compare to normal ads with just words and a picture.

# 38: BE WILLING TO INVEST IN MARKETING — PARTICULARLY ON FACEBOOK AND GOOGLE

So now we're going to go deep. Please read the following very carefully, because if you grasp the power of this, it might just change your Entrepreneurial life.

You'll notice that on the last few pages I've been encouraging you to do paid advertising on Facebook.

I haven't suggested that you do free Marketing campaigns getting people to 'like' you etc.

Why would I do that when it's so much more appealing to encourage you to do Marketing that costs nothing?

Because 99% of this 'Marketing for Free' on Facebook and Social Media is bullshit. That's why.

It doesn't work. Sorry. I wish it did. But it doesn't.

At my big seminars, I introduce dozens of my customers on stage who've managed to turn ordinary businesses into extraordinary ones. In many cases, they've gone from zero to seven figures. Not overnight but through diligently applying the 77 ways to get customers covered in this book.

In almost every case, the majority of their customers come from paid advertising on Google and Facebook. I can show you hundreds of people who've created seven figure businesses by being willing to invest in advertising on Google and Facebook.

Do you know how many I can show you who've created seven figure businesses by doing the free stuff – likes, shares etc?

None. Zero. Not one. As I said. It's all BS

Sure, we can come up with a campaign to get 50 people to like you next week on Facebook. Only problem is, that rarely leads to sales. It doesn't pay the mortgage.

It's BS perpetuated by people who want to confuse you with all this social media nonsense and charge you a fortune for complicated social media strategies that look very impressive but don't make you any money.

As a business owner, you shouldn't be easily impressed by all these statistics about how many likes and followers someone got you. To coin a phrase: "Show me the money!"

All of this requires you to undertake a change in thinking that is 180 degrees different from that of most business owners – certainly your competitors.

Everyone is obsessed about getting customers for Free. I've nothing against it. Many of the strategies we've already discussed cost nothing to implement.

But there's a difference between wanting to get customers for Free where it's the smart thing to do (such as with referrals) and refusing to engage in paid advertising because of an obsession with only getting customers that cost you nothing. It's a very false economy.

You might want to re-read that last paragraph because it contains a fundamental truth about what it takes to become wealthy as an Entrepreneur.

Every successful business owner I know sees Marketing and advertising as an investment that they are keen to make because they are looking for the best possible return on their investment.

Every struggling business owner I know sees Marketing as a cost that they want to avoid.

That's it. Want to become a Millionaire? I've just told you how. As the genius songwriter Paul Weller once said:

"If I ain't getting through, you ain't listening."

You're now in the business of buying customers. That's the road to financial freedom.

And talking of people obsessing with trying to get customers for free when it's a complete waste of time and money......

# 39: SEO IS DEAD.
# DON'T WASTE ANOTHER MINUTE ON IT

Search Engine Optimisation (SEO) is the process of manipulating Google's search engine to get your website higher up on Google's search results.

It is perhaps the biggest con ever perpetuated on the world's hardworking business owners.

SEO is dead. It is a complete waste of your time and money. Here are the FACTS that you should know about SEO:

1. Google wants its search results to be natural and 'organic.' They want those results to be a natural reflection of the popularity and relevance of websites.

2. They employ rocket scientists and have billions in the bank to stop you manipulating their search engine. The idea that Steve the SEO 'expert' down the street can beat Google and make you rich is just nonsense.

3. It is true that you can take actions that will get you higher on Google's search results, at least for a while. It's also true that if Google doesn't like those actions, they will ban you from their search engine for ever. Steve won't care. He'll just move on to his next victim.

4. Thousands of business owners have actually achieved success and made money for a while from SEO. Only problem was, when Google changed their algorithm (which

they do frequently) they woke up one morning with their website on page 23 and no business. So the irony is, if you get to the point where more than 20% of your sales came from SEO, you become horribly vulnerable anyway. You can't win either way in this game so don't bother playing it.

5.  Up to 70% of web traffic is on Mobile. Google runs four paid listings (Google pay-per-click ads) above the free listings on a phone. So even if SEO got you into third position in the free listings, you would actually be in position seven on the page on mobile. Good luck getting someone to scroll down to the seventh listing on a phone! As I said, this is all a complete waste of your time and money.

To be clear, I am a proponent of what's known as 'Natural SEO' which refers to structuring your website and online marketing so that it is in line with what Google considers when ranking search results.

This means building and structuring your website in a way that is 'Google friendly.' Also regular social media posts and encouraging genuine links to your website, so stacking the deck in your favour. But that's all.

The people who sell SEO do well because it preys on people's obsession with getting all their customers for free – and their stubborn and very stupid refusal to invest in acquiring customers.

So, if you're willing to be one of the smart ones, here's how.

# 40: THE POWER OF PAY-PER-CLICK ADVERTISING ON GOOGLE

I am about to tell you how advertising on Google Ads (formerly known as Google AdWords) took me from massive debt to my first million, changed my life, and has created more seven-figure business owners than any strategy I know.
So it's only fair that you expect me to back up such bold claims with some proof – so that you know that I know what I'm talking about.

Have a look at this. These are screenshots from the two Google Pay-per-Click accounts for my company, Cardell Media.

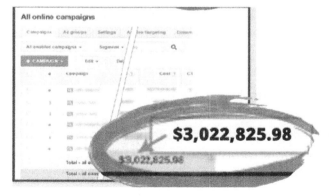

They show that I've spent almost $5 million of my own money on Google. That's £4 million.

So yes. I walk my talk.

I am the only person in the world helping business owners like you with their Google ads who has come close to spending so much of their own money on actually doing it themselves in their own business.

It's very simple: You must be doing Google Ads. There are the listings that appear above the free listings on Google.

Technically they are ads. But of course, they're really just listings. You're paying to get your site to the top of Google.

Pay-per-click advertising is the only way of reaching people who are actively looking for what you are selling. You're not chasing them, trying to convince them to become customers. They're coming to you.

This applies to business-to-consumer and business-to-business selling. It applies to both products and services. If you're a local business, it's wonderful because you can do pay-per-click advertising locally. All you have to do is specify the geographical area you want the ad to appear in.

If you've not tried this, please test Google Ads. If you've dabbled in it in the past and it has not produced the results you want, that may be because you weren't aware of some of the more advanced strategies, which we're about to cover.

**www.CardellMedia.com**

# 41: OBSESS ABOUT INCREASING YOUR CLICK-THROUGH RATE ON GOOGLE

If you're new to Google, here is what happens in a nutshell. For every 100 people who are served a page with your ad, maybe two, three, or four per cent will click on the ad. The more we can get to click, the more people will come to your website, and therefore the more customers you will get.

The percentage who click is called your Click-Through Rate or CTR.

What many businesses are not aware of is that Google rewards you for having a higher click-through rate by putting your ad further up the page. If you're already up there, it will reduce the amount of money you spend. When you get higher up the page, more people click on your ad, and you get a powerful snowball effect.

How do we increase Click-through Rate?

There are a number of ways but the best is testing different ads against each other.

Google lets you do something called 'split testing' – a fundamental part of all effective Marketing. You create two ads that are alternately served when people search for your keywords. So they are basically competing against each other to get the most clicks.

Over two, three, or four months of working on this and trying different ads you can often at least double, if not triple, your click-through rate. If you double your click-through rate, you've doubled the number of people coming to your website and coming into your business. You're higher on the page or you're paying less, so you're bringing in customers for a lot less money. You can use that money to bring in extra customers on Google or elsewhere.

This is how the cycle of success on Google begins.

# 42: DO THOROUGH KEYWORD RESEARCH

The foundation of your success on Google comes from your keywords.

Your keywords are the words which, when people search for them, Google displays your ads.

If the right keywords aren't in there, your customers won't see your listings.

If the wrong keywords are in there, you'll be paying for ineffective traffic.

How do you find the right keywords?

Part of it is common sense. Come up with a list of the obvious words and phrases that people use when discussing what you sell and that they are likely to search for on Google.

But you can also use Google to help you find the right keywords.

There's a free tool in your Google account called a 'Keyword Planner.'

Type in some of the obvious keywords and Google will show you variations and come up with suggestions of the keywords you should be testing.

The more keywords, the better (as long as they're relevant). Plus, if you're willing to write separate ads for a lot of those keywords, the ads will be more relevant and you'll get a higher Click-Through Rate, leading to more traffic and sales.

**www.CardellMedia.com**

# 43: BEYOND PAY-PER-CLICK — USE GOOGLE'S ARTIFICIAL INTELLIGENCE TO 'BUY' CUSTOMERS

I've used the phrase 'Pay-per-Click' several times here because that's how we've described Google AdWords for the last 15 year. You don't pay for your ad to appear. You only pay when someone clicks.

But actually, the days of Pay-per-Click could be coming to an end.

That's because on Google you can now pay for a sale or a lead rather than paying for the click.

It's called 'Cost per Action' or CPA bidding and is quite simply one of the most extraordinary opportunities that online marketing offers us.

With CPA bidding, you tell Google the conversions you are aiming for, which is either a sale in Ecommerce or an enquiry or phone call for a normal site.

With your Google code on your site, Google is able to measure those conversions.

Once you've had about 30 conversions, Google learns the type of people who are going to convert using all the information it has on its users and with its artificial intelligence.

As a result, Google is willing to let you pay for a result rather than a click.

So, if you're selling shoes for $200 or £200, you can tell Google that you're willing to pay, for example, $30 every time it gets a sale for you.

If you want people to fill out an enquiry form, you might tell Google you're willing to pay £10 for each enquiry.

So you are paying for results rather than clicks.

Earlier I spoke about ommission-only salespeople and how hard it is to find great salespeople who are willing to be paid purely on results.

This is Google willing to be paid purely on results. It's just one of the reasons that Google has consistently been the number-one consistent source of customers for the last 15 year for many of the world's most successful businesses.

**NOTE: It's vital that your Google advertising is managed by a world-class team. At Cardell Media, as one of the world's fastest growing digital marketing agencies, we are renowned for our results on Google, and we are an official Google partner. To find out how we can help you with your Google ads, email Profits@CardellMedia.com**

# 44: CALL TO ACTION

Make sure your ad, marketing message, or web page includes a compelling offer and a proper call to action, or "CTA." A CTA is telling people what to do. It's a really important part of any marketing piece.

Unfortunately, many salespeople and entrepreneurs often don't ask for the sale, and the same is true of many marketing pieces, websites, and ads. They could be really good, but they let themselves down at the end because they don't tell people what to do next.

If you want more customers, you need to tell your potential customers precisely what to do. Tell them, "Go to this website," or "Pick up the phone and call this number." It may sound obvious. It may even sound like it's a bit too much, but it isn't. People are busy and they often need leading. They need and want to be told what to do.

# 45: 5 ESSENTIAL STRATEGIES FOR ECOMMERCE BUSINESSES

If you have an Ecommerce business selling products online, here are five vital strategies for you to implement.

1.  The most dramatic improvements in all Ecommerce businesses can be made by improving the checkout process. It's often the case that 60% or more of people who begin the checkout process 'abandon' before they finish. You can reduce that by reducing the number of steps in the checkout process and simplifying the process as much as possible. Also, you should check your checkout process on different devices and different types of mobile phones.

2.  You must know your 'Abandonment Rate' – the percentage who begin checking out but don't finish. You or your web developer can get that info from Google Analytics.

3.  I very strongly recommend that all Ecommerce sites are built on Shopify. Unless you are very happy with your current platform, it's worth going through the hassle of moving to Shopify. It's a better Marketing platform compared to the others by factors of hundreds of per cent.

4.  Your phone number should be everywhere on your website, including on each product page. This is particularly important if you sell higher priced products. There is a percentage of the population who still want to speak to someone before buying.

5. You should set up 'Abandonment Campaigns' so that people who add to cart but don't purchase get emails and see Facebook ads specifically about the product they were looking to buy.

# 46: BANNER/DISPLAY ADVERTISING

Banner or display advertising is an increasingly interesting and important source of customers for all types of business, and it's emerging as very effective. It is underused by small and medium-sized businesses, which means there's a huge opportunity.

You see banner ads on the web pages you go to all the time. People say, "I don't pay any attention to the banner ads." You may think you don't pay attention to them, but generally people must do because it's now a multibillion-dollar industry. It used to be called banner advertising, and we now tend to call it display advertising.

There are two really important things to know about display advertising that have changed radically over the last two or three years.

First is the targeting. You can target people at very specific types of websites. If you sell handbags, you can just run your banner ads to people who visit fashion-related websites or who meet the profile of your typical customers. The targeting for display banner advertising now is incredible. The other thing is, it can be really cheap. Think of the huge inventory of web pages there are. Most people are not doing this properly, so there's a huge opportunity there for you.

If you're already doing pay-per-click advertising with Google, you do this through your Google Ads account. If you're not doing pay-per-click, you want to open a free Google Ads account with Google. You don't have to do any of the pay-per-click (although you should), but you can use your pay-per-click account for display advertising.

# 47: COMBINE ONLINE AND OFFLINE MARKETING

There's a secret that some of the big internet marketing people don't want you to know, so I'm going to tell you. I'm privileged to know some of the world's most successful online marketers, and so every now and then, about 15 or 20 of us meet for a couple of days, and we'll brainstorm what everybody is doing.

Everybody in the room is doing multimillions in terms of online selling. Everyone is obviously very good at the online stuff, like pay-per-click, Facebook, and all the rest of it. What we end up spending quite a bit of time talking about, which not everybody makes public, is how to combine traditional offline marketing with our internet marketing.

It doesn't matter how good you are at online marketing or how many great emails you send. Email open rates are 10, 20, or 30 per cent if you're lucky. That means 70 per cent or more of your customers aren't always opening your email. If we just use the internet, we're losing out big time.

The smart and wealthy internet marketers are increasingly combining online with offline marketing. By offline, I mean anything that's not online. It could be direct mail, print advertising, or getting on the phone to call people.

There are two principals to combining online and offline marketing. The first is to use offline media to get people online. You put ads in newspapers or send people direct mail or postcards to direct them to your website. You use offline media to put them online.

The other thing you want to do is get the online people offline. If I can get names and email addresses, I can put them on my email list and email them. But I really want to get their physical address as well so I can send them stuff in the mail. I'll offer an incentive or to send something in the post, like a free guide, to get customers offline as well as online.

The more you can integrate these approaches, the more you will find that your sales increase and the more customers you will bring into your business.

# 48: USE THE TELEPHONE TO INCREASE YOUR SALES

Speaking of offline marketing and traditional marketing, there's an incredible tool that so few people use in their marketing: the telephone.

Earlier we talked about getting your customers and prospects to call you, especially if they're on mobile.

But equally valuable is you calling the customers.

There are a proportion of your customers who are worth a lot more money than the rest. Most businesses have a chunk of really good customers, and they're probably willing to buy from you again. If you're not getting on the phone and communicating with them regularly, you're losing out big time.

It doesn't matter whether you want to personally call them or employ somebody to do it for you. If you hate using the phone, you shouldn't force yourself to do it if you can get somebody else to do it.

When I talk about telemarketing, I'm talking about high-value phone calls, not hard selling. I'm talking about calling people up to have a decent conversation with them.

Let's say you employed somebody full-time who was pretty good at that. They're in your business from 9 in the morning until 5 in the afternoon, five days a week. Depending on where you are and how good they are, that could cost you anything from 25,000 to 50,000 pounds or dollars a year. Let's say it's 50,000 a year because you employ an amazing telephone person who you pay with bonuses and commissions. That is 1,000 a week or 200 a day.

This person is just calling either your good customers or the people who haven't converted yet. That's all they do all day, they don't have 10-minute breaks between each call, they're constantly on the phone. If you had that person, do you think you could bring 200 pounds or dollars back into your business each day? Chances are you could probably do a lot better than that, so you will want to use telephone marketing to your advantage. It's a winner.

# 49: USE PHONE CALLS TO SERVE, NOT TO SELL

The key to using telephone marketing is to serve and not to sell. The big objection most businesses have when I talk about this is, "I don't want to pressure and pester my customers." No, you don't.

You're a customer of various businesses, both as an individual and in your own business. How many of them call you up the week after you spend money with them just to check how you're doing with what you've purchased? If they did that, wouldn't you respond positively?

If that turned into a conversation where they didn't push stuff on you but asked about what you're doing and what your needs and interests are, there's a reasonable chance you might buy from them in that phone call. If not, in the days, weeks, or months ahead you will be more predisposed to buy from them. You want to use the telephone as part of an overall strategy of adding strong value to your customers and potential customers.

# 50: ADD BONUSES

Another great way to increase sales and attract more customers is to add bonuses to your offer. Hopefully, one of the things you've learned so far is that getting customers into your business is not one-directional. There are levels of strategy, and if you work on all the levels at the same time, you will do extraordinarily well.

Some of the things we've covered so far are at the level of finding people who don't know about you yet. If you do advertising, pay-per-click, or direct mail, you're going out there and getting new customers. That's one level of doing things, but there's a whole other level we've alluded to several times, which is increasing the percentage of the people interested in what you have who are already familiar with you, who will actually buy from you. That alone is transformative for any business.

In some businesses, 90 to 95 per cent of the people who enquire never buy, so how can we get that figure higher? If we can get those conversions higher without spending any money, it's wonderful. One of the easier ways to do that is to add bonuses to incentivise people to buy. You can say, "I'm going to give you this product. The cost is xxx and I have all these bonuses to add on and give you as well."

People often laugh at infomercials, but they're worth paying attention to because it's extremely difficult to make an infomercial work. The people who do make it work put a lot of time, energy, and testing into it. If you watch carefully, one of the things they do is make the bonuses seem to be worth more than the actual product. You may have heard them say, "But wait. There's more."

If you can, add bonuses that don't cost too much money. Even if they do cost you some money, try to add some bonuses that really will incentivise and push more of your customers over the edge.

# 51: JOINT VENTURES

If you implement all of these strategies for the next ten years, you will get a lot of customers. If you and I met in ten years' time, you could tell me, "This is what we did, and we attracted 5,000 customers as a result."

But what if we could go to somebody who's already done the equivalent of that work. What if we could go to two, three, or four companies who've done the ten years of getting customers? They've put in the grind, spent the advertising money, and gotten their customers. What if we could do a joint venture with them to access those customers without having to wait?

The question to ask if you want to pursue joint ventures is (excluding competing businesses) "who already has access to the people you want to reach?"

It's kind of crazy that retail stores don't do this more often. If I'm a hairdresser and there's a beauty salon down the street, why aren't I working with the beauty salon, swapping customers, and doing joint ventures together?

Pretty much any type of company can team up with a restaurant. The restaurant goes to the local business and says, "You have access and a good relationship with these customers. If you give them this voucher for 50 per cent savings off the next meal, I'll give you free meals at the restaurant for life," or "I'll give you a 25 per cent commission," whatever it may be.

Think of people in industries that provide things around the home, like people who sell curtains, or sofas, or gardening services. Why on Earth do they not have joint ventures with the local estate agents? This stuff is not complicated. It's really straightforward, but not a lot of businesses are doing it properly.

# 52: TIME

Joint ventures are a very tangible, obvious strategy. Let's talk about a slightly more intangible but equally important one, and that's your use of time. There's a lot going on in your life that's directly linked to the number of customers you get and the amount of money you're making that may not seem so obviously linked.

As the owner of a business, whether you are a one-person business or a large business, chances are you play a key role in getting customers into your business. If we made a note of every single thing you do in your working week from when you get up in the morning until you go to sleep at night, and then we highlighted which were playing an important role in getting more customers, you would be shocked at what a small proportion of your week that is.

It is a small proportion both in terms of what you're doing, and the time spent on it. Normally, about five to ten per cent of the business owner's week is spent on getting new customers or effective marketing.

It's not that the other things you're doing aren't necessary or even important. The question is whether they should be done by you. I would suggest that getting customers is the most important thing in your business. Therefore, getting better at it is the most important thing in your business. If we could take care of that, providing you have a good product or service, everything else falls in place.

**www.CardellMedia.com**

You want to be very focused on the use of your time. Unless your business is in this extraordinary place where it's already making tons of money for you, you want to start getting quite ruthless about anything using up your time that is not helping get more customers into your business.

Start getting ruthless about using your time wisely. You might need to make some tough decision about anything you're doing in your business that doesn't involve getting new customers.

If you're going to carry on doing a specific activity, you must be pretty certain nobody else can do it or that you can't outsource it to somebody else. You may start letting things go, and they may not be done quite as well as they used to be done by you. That doesn't matter. The pursuit of perfection is ironically not always an Entrepreneurial strength. My strong advice is that you should spend at least 50 per cent of your time working on getting new customers into your business or creating processes to do so.

# 53: EXPAND YOUR GEOGRAPHY

So far, most of what we have covered has been about doing what you currently do in exactly the way you currently do it but doing the marketing better. That's great, and you want to be doing all that, but next, I want to expand your thinking a little bit.

Chances are you are selling what you are selling in a limited geography. You may be a local business, and you're selling within a few miles of where you're based. You may be a regional business, and you sell within your region. You may sell nationally. You may even sell to some other countries. Whichever one of those categories you fall into, if I were to ask you if you can sell what you sell in other geographic areas, chances are the answer is yes.

If you're serving an area that has a certain population and we could double, triple, or multiply by a factor of ten the population you service or sell to, that would be a great way of bringing in more customers. What about doubling, tripling, or quadrupling the customers you bring into your business?

One of my big messages to entrepreneurs is that wealth is a choice. The amount of money you have in your bank account is a choice. Everybody thinks the world decides how much money you've got. Well, not at the level you're playing at. Once you're a smart, marketing-savvy entrepreneur, wealth is a choice. What choices are you making about how much money you earn? You might not want to sell to the whole country. You might not want to sell to Europe and America. That's fine, but it's a choice. Consider expanding your geography.

# 54: EXPAND YOUR PRODUCTS

Consider expanding your products. There's a truth about every single business out there. If we took your top 20 or 30 per cent of customers, there's almost certainly stuff they're not buying from you now that they would be willing to buy if you offered it to them.

What you see might be directly related to your current product or service, or it might be something unrelated. When I discussed joint ventures, I asked why estate agents aren't teaming up with all the other home-related companies. It works both ways. The sofa company, the curtain company, and the gardening company are a bit daft for not teaming up with the estate agent.

The estate agent, if they were willing to effectively expand their product base, would benefit incredibly. The estate agent will tell you, "I can't expand my products because I only have one thing I sell. I sell houses, and people live in a house for eight years. There's nothing I can do." This is nonsense. The real power in your business is the relationship you have with your customers, and we're talking about leveraging that relationship. Come up with something new to sell them and you'll make more money. It's a very powerful way to expand a business.

# 55: EXPAND YOUR ENTREPRENEURIAL HORIZONS

If you want to get really into this, expand your entrepreneurial horizons. When you made the decision to go into the business you're currently in, you probably didn't know what you now know about marketing. If you're on a path of learning, certainly you're going to know more in three months, six months, a year, or two years down the line.

If you were to go back to the point where you set up your business in the first place, if you knew then what you know now, would you pick that business? Would you pick that business and other businesses? Would you pick totally different businesses? A lot of serial entrepreneurs become very wealthy. Remember that you always have the choice to do more and to do different things with the skill that you have.

As an entrepreneur, you can now apply your marketing skills in all sorts of arenas. You could do it with your existing business or your new business, and/or you could team up with others to do it. The world is yours to choose from.

I'm not encouraging you to open 23 businesses if that's not your thing. I spend most of my time turning down offers to do extra stuff because I'm very focused on what I want to do with my time. I don't want to get into the loop a lot of successful entrepreneurs get into, which is that they just can't say no. What I'm talking about is the theme here, to reach more customers. Has it crossed your mind that one of the ways to do that is to reach customers from totally unrelated businesses? It's an interesting thought.

# 56: TEST PERMISSION MARKETING

Permission marketing, rather than marketing that sells to people straightaway, is marketing that gets a customer's permission to begin a relationship with them. It is a fundamentally different form of marketing than most marketing, but it plays a big part in what I do and what a lot of our business owners that we work with do.

In a lot of arenas, it's too much to ask people who don't know you to spend money with you. The classic example is a website. If someone who didn't know you two minutes ago arrives at your website, the chances of you getting money out of them are slim. Specifically, less than 1 per cent of people who visit a typical website will buy from that website.

If you use a permission marketing model, you can say to visitors to your website, "You didn't know me 30 seconds ago, but I have some really interesting, useful information. I've put it on a free online video for you. Just give me your name and email address, and here it is." Instead of a 1 per cent response, you'll probably get a 5% to 15% response rate.

Permission marketing is great because then the customer watches your video, they're really into you, and they probably will contact you anyway. If they don't, you've got their email address, and you can follow up with them.

# 57: MEASURE AND TEST YOUR MARKETING

Testing is the foundation of all marketing. It directly relates to getting more customers into your business. The basic principle is you want to test all your marketing. First, you want to test new marketing methods, like some of the ones I've been offering you here.

When we do any form of marketing, like the pay-per-click ads, we want to test different ads to improve the response. Any form of testing that improves the result of your marketing brings you more customers. If you're running a successful ad in a newspaper or magazine, test it with a completely different headline. If that gives you a 15 per cent increase in customers, there you go. You must measure and test all of your marketing.

# 58: THE 80/20 PRINCIPLE AND PROFILING

This is a more advanced strategy, but you definitely want to do this. In a downturn, it's essential that you focus on your best customers.

The 80/20 principle applies in virtually every business. We find that about 20 per cent of your customers generate about 80 per cent of your profits. There are all sorts of reasons for this. We don't need to go into them here, but it's a very standard rule. It can vary a bit, maybe it's 70/30 or 85/15, but the point is it's never evenly proportionate to the effort you put in. Not all of your customers are worth the same to you. There's a chunk of your customers who are worth more, normally a lot more.

You want to be looking for the customers who are most likely to give you money in the weeks and months ahead. You will find them in the 20% who bring in 80% of your profits. Hone in on them and focus on them with laser like precision.

This also applies to new customer acquisition. If not all customers are created the same, you don't just want anyone as a new customer. You want those good buyers.

Let's suppose you acquired 1,000 customers over time, and of those 1,000 customers, 80 per cent of the profits in your business only came from 20 per cent of them. We can go out there and get another 1,000 customers, which is great because that would double the size of your business, but what if the next 1,000 customers all came from the same category of that 20 per cent? I can't even do the maths on what that would do to your business. It would be incredible.

This is another area where Facebook excels. Earlier, I mentioned lookalike audiences. You can go a step further and just upload your top 20% of customers and ask Facebook to go and find people who look like them. The results can be extremely profitable.

# 59: NETWORKING

When you talk to business owners, one of the things that always happens is they stop taking the actions they did at the beginning that was really successful for them. It's understandable because you end up busy doing 101 other things.

In the early days of a business, most business owners have to sell their wares wherever they can. You want to be out there interacting and networking with fellow human beings as much as you can. It is one of the most obvious but underused ways to get more customers.

This is going to depend on what you sell. If you sell to consumers, where are the consumers? Where can you hang out with them? If you sell to businesses, where can you hang out at business breakfasts or whatever it might be? Do things really well when it comes to networking or mixing.

Obviously in the current climate a lot of networking has moved online – but that's a reason to do more of it. Networking without travel. Perfect.

# 60: PUBLIC RELATIONS

Before we go spending  on advertising, how about getting advertising for free in the form of free PR, or public relations. It's a great open book sitting there for business owners.

There's a core principle for you to understand about PR. Everybody thinks it's difficult to get into the media, but actually the opposite is the case. I used to work in media. I used to work in radio, so I know exactly how it works.

In any newspaper or magazine or on any radio or TV station, there are producers or journalists almost pulling their hair out because they have to fill hours of radio or TV time or pages in newspapers and magazines. They have to fill it with interesting people and interviews, and that's hard to find.

For example, when you're looking to fill a radio show that has some speech content on it, not only have you got to find a subject that's interesting and somebody who knows what they're talking about, but that person has to be able to communicate and be somewhat eloquent.

There are things you know about; either the type of business you're in, the product you sell, or the arena you work in that segments of the population out there are also interested in. Providing you're able to meet the needs of the producer or journalist on the other end, you will find they are far more receptive than you might think to giving you PR coverage.

Let's talk about some specifics on how to do that.

**www.CardellMedia.com**

# 61: THE "5 TOP TIPS" PRESS RELEASE

This is a real PR secret for you that is simple and straightforward. Whenever I'm advising somebody on getting started with PR, I tell them to try the "5 Top Tips" press release strategy. This hardly ever fails.

There's something you're an expert on. Let's say you're an accountant, and it's budget time. You could go to your local media with five top tips for cutting your taxes, saving for retirement, or retiring early. If you sell office supplies, you could go to the local media, to certain business-to-business publications, or to the business section of The Sunday Times and say, "Here's a great story for you. How about the five top tips on creating the perfect productive and relaxing workspace?" Put all this into a press release and come up with your five top tips.

Why does this work so well? Think about what I said about these producers and journalists. They're looking for a good story. The five top tips thing is literally handing them their story on a plate. They will write an article or produce a radio feature around these five top tips. It's also really useful for you because when you get on the media or if you're interviewed, you have your five bullet points to talk about. The "5 Top Tips" press release works really well.

# 62: PREMIUM PRICING

Everybody tends to assume that putting your prices up or selling more expensive stuff can have a detrimental effect on your ability to get more customers. That's not the case. There is a segment of the population reluctant to spend money on products or services that appear too cheap.

By premium pricing, I mean a more expensive and more high-end version. If you sell shoes and your average shoe is £50, make sure you have a £500 or £600 option in there. You won't lose anything because if you keep the lower-priced option, you'll keep the customers you get that way. The addition of a premium-priced option can actually bring you in new and more customers who you would not have reached in the first place.

If I'm looking for a product or service or someone to help me with a certain area in my business, I'm going to think twice if it's too cheap. Suppose I want the world's greatest YouTube expert to work on my business. If I hear recommendations, and finally find somebody who tells me their rate is $10 an hour, I will question whether they're good enough to do what I want doing because shouldn't they be charging more than that?

The whole art of pricing is fascinating because when you set your prices higher and move to a more high-end business, it helps convey a completely new level of doing business. Premium pricing can be a customer acquisition strategy, and very few people understand that.

# 63: PAYMENT PLANS

If you are able and willing to give your customers the option to pay in monthly instalments, you will normally see an increase in sales in at least the 20 to 40 per cent range. If you normally have a one-off payment and you let customers pay over two or three months, that will normally give you a significant increase in sales, depending on where you are priced at the moment. If you sell particularly high-end expensive products or services, you can extend that to even longer.

Just splitting a payment into two or three changes the perception because the customer will be very focused on that monthly payment amount, rather than the total amount. Making higher priced products and services more affordable without reducing your costs is a very effective strategy.

# 64: THE AIDA PRINCIPLE

There is a core principle in all marketing for attracting more customers that works everywhere. This will work on your website, sales letters, brochures, emails, and in actual conversations with potential customers. The AIDA principle is the formula a customer goes through in their head that leads to them buying. The more you can direct that process to occur, the more money you'll make because the more sales you'll get.

AIDA stands for Attention, Interest, Desire, and Action. If I arrive at your web page, there'd better be a compelling headline that grabs my attention and keeps me reading. You need to keep my interest, or I'm gone. Interest isn't enough though. It's not enough for me to read and be interested in your newspaper or magazine ad. You need to turn the interest into a desire. Get people wanting something. You are 80 per cent there once you have the desire, but that's still not enough. There are a lot of things people want, but do they actually take action and get them? You now need to turn all that desire into action.

If you start talking to your customers about taking action and buying something from you but you don't have their interest or desire, you've missed an important step.

If you're on the phone to a customer, or if they're physically with you and you feel that you're losing them a bit, ask yourself where you are in the AIDA process. Maybe go back to the interest point. Use this principle in all of your marketing.

# 65: MULTIPLE FOLLOW-UP

Businesses don't follow up anything like enough on their prospects and customers.

Go and watch Glengarry Glenross. Work those leads until they buy, die, or tell you to go away. The principal way to do that is with multiple follow-ups, because most businesses give up far too easily.

Let's say somebody emails or phones you about what you have to offer and you have a record of who they are. Most people will reply to the email or phone the person up, and maybe they'll send something in the post or send an email with additional information attached. In other words, they'll follow up with that customer once or twice. That is what 90 per cent of businesses do.

There have been so many interesting studies on this. It's been researched again and again. On average, if you do multiple follow-ups properly, it takes seven points of contact to convert a lead, a potential customer who has inquired with you, into a buying customer.

The form of contact is going to vary slightly depending on the business you're in, but the principle is always the same. On average, your customer is going to need an email, another email, maybe a phone call, maybe another email, maybe something in the post, maybe a face-to-face meeting if it's appropriate for you, maybe another email or two, and only then do they become a customer.

I ask a question at our Entrepreneur Summit, and the answer never fails to amaze me. I ask, "Who's been on my email list for three years, and this is the first time you've actually spent any money with me?" Every year, there are 30, 40, and sometimes 50 people who raise their hand. If they've been on my email list for three years, they've probably had 150 to 200 emails from me. Most businesses and entrepreneurs give up at just one or two.

You absolutely need to do multiple follow-ups. If somebody comes within a mile of your business, you want to have a system in place for this, whether it be email, direct mail, telephone calls, or other forms of good marketing.

# 66: RADIO ADVERTISING

Radio advertising can be a great part of the marketing mix, particularly for a growing business and particularly if you have a strong local or regional presence. There are lots of businesses who created themselves off the back of good radio advertising. If you're a national business, it's something to test doing nationally.

You need to be careful because it's easy to spend a lot of money, and you don't want to do that without getting any return. It's certainly worth doing low-cost tests on the radio, especially if you are a local or regional business. Local radio reaches a good percentage of the population. If it's done right and you're not paying over the odds, it can be a worthwhile strategy.

Whatever price they tell you – halve it. If you buy radio advertising on the rate cards these radio stations try to offer, you'll be paying far too much money.

Radio advertising is something to test, but please follow our golden rule: You must test and measure all your advertising. Radio advertising, like all marketing, is well worth testing.

# 67: USE YOUR CONTACT LIST

Using your contact list is a strategy that's overlooked. You and the people in your business have a network of people in your phone books or mobile phones, and that is your contact list. Within that contact list, you have people who might become customers or people with access to potential customers.

When I talk about your contact list, I encourage you to look at yourself, your life, and your history, and all the people you've ever had contact and good relations with.

One of the things that most successful, wealthy entrepreneurs are very good at is tapping in to the people they know or the people who know the people they know, even if some of those links are tentative. If we have a relationship with somebody, or a relationship with somebody through somebody else, and we're asked a favour, most of the time we will do it.

If you're trying to get access to a certain type of business, a specific person in a business, or certain types of people to reach as customers, take a good strong look at your contact list. There are people you could contact if you needed to, either personally or by phone, email, Facebook, or whatever it is. Ask yourself who in that list could be a customer or potential customer.

The network marketing industry, which I am not a huge fan of, is a big industry that makes a lot of money. It doesn't always make a lot of money for most of the people in it, but that's a story for another day. One of the ways they do this is to convince the new member, the new person selling their vitamins, health products, or whatever it may be to tap in to their network of people.

Obviously, you want to implement the more advanced marketing and advertising we've covered here, but isn't it a bit silly to not first tap into your own existing contact list? Have a think about that and focus on areas or people within that list that you can tap in to. Think of colleagues of colleagues or friends of friends. If you know someone whose sister is in that industry, go for it. Being an entrepreneur, you have to push the boat a little and sometimes go beyond your comfort zone. This is important because it doesn't matter how great your product or service is if nobody knows about it or buys it.

# 68: NICHE

Niching is such a great source of potential new customers. It involves something fundamental about how people buy. People will be more inclined to buy from a company that is more focused on their specific needs.

Suppose you needed heart surgery. You had a choice of two good surgeons. All Surgeon 1 does is the particular heart surgery you need. It's complicated, but they do it every day. In fact, they've done it for the last ten years day in and day out, and they can do it with their eyes closed. Surgeon 2 is an equally good surgeon, maybe an even better surgeon, with an outstanding reputation. Surgeon 2 has a gift that they can do hearts, legs, knees, brains, and anything at all. Every couple of weeks, they'll do heart surgery, and every now and then they'll do the type of surgery you need.

Which surgeon would you pick? You're probably going to pick the first one because they have gone into a niche. So as consumers or buyers, we are more inclined toward that niche.

This is something to start thinking about within your business. It doesn't mean you have to stop or change what you're doing necessarily, but you may want to introduce elements of your business that are just for that niche.

Financial advisors can advise on mortgages or insurance, and maybe they work on helping business owners get loans. They have that skill and ability. If I was doing the marketing for one of those businesses, the first thing I would do is divide them up.

I would have them as separate entities, possibly with separate names and certainly with separate websites.

If you are looking for insurance as a business owner, the website you end up at is a website just about insurance for business owners. It's not also about mortgages and this, that, and the other. There's no great logical reason to that because there's no reason somebody can't multitask, but we're just more comfortable with a niched offering. Your sales will increase if you target a niche.

If you fix cars for a living, and you move into a new city where you set up a garage fixing cars, one of your challenges is you're the new person, and there are 27 other garages in town. Why on Earth should they come to you? If you're willing to be the person who focuses on just fixing BMWs and you set up a BMW-fixing garage, you narrow your market, but it makes the sales message to that customer so much easier. It also makes the customer easy to find. All you have to do is market to BMW owners, and you can get mailing lists of BMW owners.

How could you niche in your business? How you do this is up to you, but it makes the marketing a lot easier if you can just go for specific people and reach certain people within that arena.

# 69: BUNDLING

You can bundle the products you offer together to create packages, to increase sales. If I owned a camera shop selling digital camera stuff, I could measure how many people buy from me. Maybe one out of ten spends on average £70 or £80 on a camera. I could try not changing anything that's already working, but additionally have a bundled option. If they want, they could get the camera in a bundle, with a tripod and a lovely full colour book with 101 photography tips for just £99.

Bundling works because it greatly increases the perceived value. Suddenly, I'm not just getting a camera. I'm getting the camera, the tripod, and the book. Combined, that has a reasonably good perceived value for only £10 or £20 more than the customer was paying for the camera.

If you do this properly, it's not going to cost you much more. You may not even make additional profits per sale. In other words, you might give them the tripod and the book at cost price, but what if that gets two people out of ten instead of one person out of ten who come into the shop to buy from you?

Consider how you can bundle. You can do this with services too, we're not just talking about physical products. When a free service warranty is added onto a product, that is a form of bundling. When postage, packing, and shipping is added on free to a product, that is a form of bundling.

That shift in the perception of that first product can really make a difference to your sales, so it's well worth testing.

# 70: RESHAPE YOUR CORE PRODUCT OR SERVICE

Unless you're a huge retailer or online retailer, most businesses have one, two, or maybe three main products or services the new customer buys, even if you have a range of offers you sell them down the road. Reshaping or changing either the amount, quantity, or quality of that first offering can have very interesting consequences on sales.

When we test any new marketing method – an ad, internet advert, or something on a website – we can test the copy, headlines, or price. One of the first things we want to test is the actual offer. Customers will respond very differently to small, discreet shifts and changes in that core product in ways that are very hard to predict.

Whenever you test this, you tend to see very different responses to different types of products and different price points. It's almost impossible for you as the business owner to be the best judge of what that should be because you're too close to your business. It's worth testing and trying that out, so play around with this. Step into the shoes of a new customer. Have a look at what you're offering them as the first thing to buy. Test variations on that.

You can test a bigger, more expensive thing. That can be very interesting to do because sometimes you can get an increase in price without losing your sales rate, which is great because it's giving you more money immediately. Sometimes a reduction in price will double, triple, or quadruple those early sales. Remember, we're buying customers. We're bringing customers in through the door. Reshaping your core product or service is a good way to get sales.

We've done some advanced strategies, and now I'm going to give you a really advanced one. Virtually nobody does this, but if you are willing enough, smart enough, and persistent enough to do this, this is a brilliant strategy for getting customers.

# 71: OTHER BUSINESSES' NON-BUYERS

This seems counterintuitive, which is why so few people are willing to do it. You say to your competitors, "We're competitors, and that's fine. Think about this for a minute. You spend money on marketing and advertising. You have a website and all the rest of it. Some people contact you but don't become customers. You've spent good money trying to get those people. You've basically paid for non-buyers. I'm in the same position. My non-buyers aren't going to buy from me, and yours aren't going to buy from you. How about we make some money out of this and give each other access to the non-buyers?"

Sometimes people just won't buy from you for whatever reason, but we know they had an interest in the product or service. Maybe you just weren't right for them. If someone different comes along with a different offering, it's a really cool strategy. It's a little bit like joint ventures. You'll immediately get access to people who are that close to becoming customers, and you're not losing because you're giving the competitor access to people who probably aren't going to buy from you anyway.

To pull this off, you need some tenacity. You need to be persistent because most of the competitors will initially be reluctant.

Watch the huge multibillion-pound or multibillion-dollar companies, particularly in the tech world. Apple, Microsoft, Google, and Facebook all compete with each other at certain levels, yet they tend to have simultaneous cooperative relationships.

Don't rule out cooperating with your competition. Normally the pie is big enough for everybody.

# 72: BECOME AN AUTHORITY — CLAIM THE LEADERSHIP POSITION

As you go through these strategies, there are a couple of things that will make a difference to all of them working well.

One of them is the extent to which you or your business is regarded as an authority in the marketplace. You want to claim the leadership position because in any type of business or arena, there is a leader.

If I say "fizzy cola drink," you probably think Coca-Cola. If you're in Britain and I say "a really famous hypnotist," you probably think of Paul McKenna. There are other cola drinks out there, and there are thousands of hypnotists, but Paul McKenna and Coca-Cola have established themselves in the leadership position.

I mention Paul specifically because I know him. We worked together on a radio station a long time ago before I was doing this and before he was doing what he now does. I know for a fact that he decided to establish that leadership position and started pushing himself forward as a leader in that field before he'd done all the things that would naturally have him labelled as a leader. He either understood intuitively or he learned that if you wait for somebody to label you as leader, often you will have a very long wait.

Some of our members and customers have done very well. When I go to their websites, I smile because I see the phrase "Britain's leading wedding photographer" or "Europe's leading manufacturer of screwdrivers" or "America's leading real estate agent," whatever it may be.. They've claimed that leadership position.

If you're willing to be bold – and you do need to have a bit of boldness as an entrepreneur – you want to claim that leadership. Someone is going to claim it in your industry if they haven't already. Why not you?

# 73: BECOME AN AUTHORITY — WRITE A BOOK

The businesses that come out of Recessions thriving do so partly because either the business – or the owner of that business – is regarded as the authority in their market. They are perceived as superior to the competition by the customers.

There are various ways to establish yourself as the authority in your sector – but the fastest way is to write and self-publish a book.

The purpose of producing a book is not to get into a bookstore. The purpose is to have your customers see you're an author of a book, which gives you instant credibility. Secondly, you can use that book as a marketing tool. You'll often see smart marketers giving away books as a free gift on their website or in their ads.

Writing a book is wonderful because it has several immediate impacts. It helps credibility and authority, but it's also a great early sales or lead generation tool.

Everybody can write a book. There's information and knowledge you have about the work that you do that your customers want to know about. An architect can do a book showing the amazing homes they work on. A manufacturer can produce a book with top tips for using what they manufacture. I have a book called '77 Ways To Get More Customers' that you may be familiar with! A significant proportion of people who read this book end up becoming long-term clients because it's immediately clear to them that my team and I know what we're doing, have a proven track record, and can have a major impact on their business.

You can either write the book yourself, use a ghost writer, or have someone interview you and turn that into your book.

Then you can self-publish as many copies as you want: 20, 50, 100, 10,000. It's up to you.

Again, the value of this is not actually in how many people get or read your book. It's that you are now a published author – a leader in the field – and you have a great advantage over the competition.

Becoming the authority in your market also helps with pricing. We constantly see the business where the owner is the author of 'the book' and is able to command prices significantly higher than the competition.

# 74: CONSIDER SCALING UP YOUR MARKETING DURING THE RECESSION

If you have access to cash, you should seriously consider scaling up your Marketing during this Recession.

Cost per click on Facebook and Google is plummeting. Your competitors are disappearing. Sadly, many of those competitors will go out of business. We can hate the economic situation while simultaneously acknowledging that this is a major opportunity for smart Entrepreneurs.

Anyone who knows about the world of investing knows that the time to buy is in a downturn. If you understand that Marketing is the process of investing to buy leads and customers, now is the time to buy, if you can.

So with my clients, we have Ecommerce companies increasing their budgets by 100% or more in this Recession. We have physical stores converting to Ecommerce sites in a few days. We have B2B companies changing their websites to lead generation sites.

Just because everyone around you is panicking doesn't mean that you have to. If you see even an ounce of opportunity in the months ahead, seize it.

# 75: ACTION AND IMPLEMENTATION

This is the foundation on which everything is built. Hopefully, you understand that you have more than enough strategies now to get as many customers as you want. Why wouldn't you go out there and get them? The only reason that you would not succeed at this is by not acting and not obsessing about implementation.

If you're smart enough and determined enough to still be reading this far, please don't let yourself down by not taking action, by not implementing these marketing strategies in your business. This is all about implementation. You don't have to be a great or experienced marketer; you just need to be willing to take action, and more action than anybody else.

Remember the importance of this subject here. You're not actually here because all you want is more customers. You're not even really here because all you want is more customers to help the company grow.

The truth of the matter is you're a business owner. As a business owner, everything financially in your life, the financial wellbeing of yourself and maybe your family, and the property you own all depends on your ability to get customers.

I hope you're inspired and excited at the opportunity here. Please do something with that excitement and inspiration. Take action.

We have two strategies to go. The first one is an important psychological mindset strategy. The final one is a very specific strategy that will make you oodles of money. I've saved one of the best until last.

# 76: UNDERSTAND THE REAL BUSINESS YOU'RE IN

If I was to say to you before today, "What business are you in?" or you came to a seminar and asked everybody in the room one by one, "What business are you in?" you'd probably get 200 different answers from the 200 different people in the room. "I'm in the wedding industry," "I'm in the manufacturing business," "I'm an internet web designer." But that's not the real business that you're in.

The real business you're in is marketing. The real business you're in as an entrepreneur is getting customers. Unfortunately, we take for granted the quality of the product or service we provide. Obviously, that needs to be in place, but that's like getting up in the morning. It has to happen anyway. That's not the real business you're in, or what will determine your success or failure, or the level of success you experience. The thing that will determine your success is how many customers you get, and the thing that's going to determine how many customers you get is your marketing.

The real business you are in is marketing, so you should start every day focusing on that. This loops back to one of our earlier points when we looked at time. I would reinforce the message that the amount of time you are willing to spend on marketing is a vital part of all of this because that's the business you're in.

Let me give you a really cool strategy to round off with. This is so simple, straightforward, and obvious. It is the real untapped profits that sit in every business, but virtually nobody does it.

# 77: REACTIVATE OLD/LOST CUSTOMERS

We said earlier that one of the fastest ways to grow a business is to sell more to existing customers. If we want to give a business an instant cash boost, we start talking to the existing customers because they're so much easier to sell to than new customers.

But the next best group to contact are your old customers who are not buying from you anymore. They are customers who are still there in the mix but have stopped buying from you or you stopped making offers to them, or they're lost customers in the sense that they were customers of yours once, and they're not customers of yours anymore. They've gone away, and they're spending money with somebody else. You have a great opportunity to reactivate these ex-customers.

If you have a new business and are not in this position yet, please make a big note of this because this is going to be one you absolutely want to implement. Reactivating customers who aren't spending money with you, for whatever reason, is one of the real delights of marketing because everyone is pleasantly surprised with the results.

Understand that if people have stopped spending money with you, it rarely has anything to do with you, apart from the fact that maybe you're not communicating with them enough.

Generally speaking, people stop buying from a business because the business ignores them. It is quite likely you've ignored people who have spent money with you three months ago, three years ago, or maybe even longer. If you're willing to reactivate them, you'll be very happy with how many come back.

If you've not paid enough attention to them, apologise. Say, "I've been thinking about it, and I don't think I've paid enough attention to you. I haven't contacted you over the last few months. I've not been checking how you are. I just want to check in with you. How are things going? Is there anything I can do for you?"

If you think you've lost them to somebody else, one of the great marketing letters goes along these lines. "Dear Julie," or "Dear John, was it something I said? Was it something I did? I'm shocked that I may have upset or offended you. If I have, I deeply apologise.

"I value your business, and I miss you. If I've done something to let you down, I would really like to know what that is so I can put it right. If it's just that time has gone by and we haven't been in contact, I'd like to re-establish our relationship and let you know how important you are to me. I'm just checking in to see how you're doing."

When did anybody last say that or anything similar to you? It doesn't happen, does it? Like all the strategies we've talked about here today, it's simple and straightforward. It can be profoundly profitable, but virtually nobody does it.

Whether you're self-employed, an up-and-coming entrepreneur, or the owner of a small, medium, or large business, I have a simple message for you: Wealth is a choice. It's really down to you now on the number of these 77 strategies you are willing to implement.

Bear in mind that if you tried one every week, then in a year and a half, you'd have 77 new approaches to your business and your business will be absolutely transformed.

Thank you for spending this time with me and for investing this time in yourself. I would love to hear your success stories, so please do get in touch.

Good luck with it all. Take massive action and reap the rewards.

# THE NEXT STEP

If you need help implementing world-class Marketing in your business, my company, Cardell Media, is one of the world's fastest growing Digital Marketing agencies. We work with business owners across the world including UK, USA, Canada, Australia,  and New Zealand. We can help you create a world-class website and look after your key Online Marketing activities. Check out the information on the following pages, then email us at **Profits@CardellMedia.com**

We look forward to partnering with you to create the success that you deserve.

**Chris Cardell**

# CARDELL MEDIA WEBSITE AND INTERNET MARKETING PARTNERSHIP

This is your complete website solution. Our team will build you a powerful, conversion-driven website using the latest technologies. We will also take care of your online video, all of your social media – and give you personal support in the months and years ahead with a dedicated Account Manager. Whether you are in B2B, sell services, or you require a sophisticated Ecommerce site, we can help. Check out what is included below, and then contact us to see how we can take your business to the next level:

## HERE'S WHAT'S INCLUDED IN YOUR WEBSITE AND INTERNET MARKETING PARTNERSHIP

### WEBSITE MARKETING - DESIGN & BUILD

- A Profit-Driven, Direct Response new website. We will build you a new website or redesign your current website (Up to a maximum of 25 pages)
- A complete mobile-friendly website
- Your new mobile website will be built on the Cardell Media X2 Mobile Platform
- Speed. We aim to complete your website and home page video within 30 – 60 days
- Install the Cardell Media Email Autoresponder on your Website

### VIDEO

- Our media team will produce a home page video
- Host your online video on state-of-the-art video hosting
- Produce up to two additional videos for you each year

**SUPPORT**

- Two years of Unlimited Support with your dedicated Account Manager
- Create up to five additional web pages each month for two years
- Fast, efficient support. Two years of website management. Make any changes required to existing pages
- Two Years Free membership of Chris Cardell's VIP Inner Circle

**HOSTING**

- Two years hosting on our high security, dedicated servers
- Secure Sites - our sites include an SSL Certificate to encrypt client data and protect you
- 24/7/365 managed hosting. If something goes wrong, our team are monitoring and fixing
- Built-in staging environments to ensure edits are tested before going live
- Daily back up, so your data is always safe
- Managed Patching & Updates
- Dedicated Cardell Hosting Environment servers

**SOCIAL & OPTIMISATION**

- Natural SEO, including Google XML site submission, H1, H2 and Meta Tags, SEO check
- Social media posts and social media account linking
- Create or redesign your Facebook business page
- Create or redesign your LinkedIn business page
- Create or redesign your Instagram page
- Write and post weekly posts for two years on Facebook
- Write and post weekly posts for two years on LinkedIn
- Write and post weekly posts for two years on Instagram

## To find out how we can help you, email Profits@CardellMedia.com

# CARDELL MEDIA GOOGLE ADS AND ONLINE ADVERTISING PARTNERSHIP

The world's finest Online Marketing team at Cardell Media will take your business to the next level using the finest in Google Ads management, Remarketing, Bing/Yahoo, YouTube, In Market and Custom Intent ads.

## HERE'S WHAT'S INCLUDED IN YOUR GOOGLE ADS AND ONLINE ADVERTISING PARTNERSHIP

### FULL GOOGLE ADS MANAGEMENT

- Carry out a full Audit of your Google Ads account or set up your new account if you're new to Google advertising.
- Make sure that your Account and Campaign Structure is set up to maximise profits
- Full Artificial Intelligence and Machine Learning management
- Keyword Research
- Write your ads based on our knowledgebase and results from creating over 10,000 Google ads
- Ongoing Ad Creation, Testing, and Management
- Set up ongoing ad split testing
- Create and Manage Ad Extensions
- Manage Campaign Budgets and Bid Strategy
- Set up and manage Conversion tracking
- Manage and Optimise your account each month using the proven Cardell Search Marketing Optimisation Process
- Bidding Strategies
- Mobile Google Ads Strategy
- Match Type Management
- RLSA
- Geographic Bidding Options

- Dayparting
- Conversion Tracking and Management
- Google Shopping
- Impression Share Management
- Top Position Management
- Monthly Reporting
- Dedicated Account Manager

**GOOGLE REMARKETING**
- Google Display Remarketing campaign set up
- Audience selection and tracking
- Banner ad creation
- Google's new Responsive Ad creation and management
- Remarketing campaign bidding, management and reporting

**FACEBOOK REMARKETING**
- Facebook Remarketing campaign set up
- Facebook ad creation
- Audience selection
- Bidding management
- Conversion goal selection, tracking, and management
- Full management, and reporting

**YOUTUBE REMARKETING**
- YouTube Remarketing campaign set up
- Audience selection
- Ad Creation
- Machine Learning management
- YouTube Remarketing bidding, management and reporting

## To find out how we can help you, email Profits@CardellMedia.com

Made in the USA
Coppell, TX
21 January 2023

11461250R10079